to

from

date

DRAWING STRENGTH FROM THE
NAMES OF GOD

CATHERINE MARTIN

HARVEST HOUSE PUBLISHERS

EUGENE, OREGON

Drawing Strength from the Names of God

Text Copyright © 2010 by Catherine Martin

Photography Copyright © Steve Terrill

Published by Harvest House Publishers

Eugene, Oregon 97402

www.harvesthousepublishers.com

ISBN 978-0-7369-2578-5

Design and production by Left Coast Design, Portland, Oregon

Unless otherwise indicated, Scripture quotations are taken from the New American Standard Bible®, © 1960, 1962, 1963, 1968, 1971, 1972, 1973, 1975, 1977, 1995 by The Lockman Foundation. Used by permission. (www.Lockman.org). Verses marked NIV are taken from the HOLY BIBLE, NEW INTERNATIONAL VERSION®. NIV®. Copyright ©1973, 1978, 1984 by the International Bible Society. Used by permission of Zondervan. All rights reserved. Verses marked TNIV are taken from the Holy Bible, Today's New International Version® (TNIV®) Copyright © 2001 by International Bible Society. All rights reserved worldwide. Verses marked NKJV are taken from the New King James Version. Copyright ©1982 by Thomas Nelson, Inc. Used by permission. All rights reserved.

All rights reserved. No part of this publication may be reproduced, stored in a retrieval system, or transmitted in any form or by any means—electronic, mechanical, digital, photocopy, recording, or any other—except for brief quotations in printed reviews, without the prior permission of the publishers.

Printed in China.

10 11 12 13 14 15 / LP / 10 9 8 7 6 5 4 3 2 1

Draw Strength from Elohim —He Is Your Creator

In the beginning God created the heavens and the earth.

Genesis 1:1

Genesis is the book of beginnings, and Elohim is the Author of all beginnings. He is outside the realm of time, wholly other and infinite. And yet, intensely personal, He has chosen to create. Elohim created the heavens and the earth, and even more profoundly, He created you. Do you long to understand who you are, why you are here, and what your purpose is in life? Because God created you, you have personal worth and significance. Knowing you are created in the image of God for His glory answers a thousand questions in your life. You can know, because you are created in the image of God, that God has attached an intrinsic value and worth to you; He has created you for a purpose—for His glory.

Your life is meant to show the greatness and glory and, in fact, the very presence and existence of God.

The heavens declare the glory of God; the skies proclaim the work of his hands.

Psalm 19:1 TNIV

Draw Near to Elohim

If you have moments when you question the reality of God or His nearness, open your front door, walk outside, and look at God's creation. Look up at the sky, look out at the birds, trees, and fields, and look down at the intricacy of your hand. Then declare, "Elohim, You created the heavens and the earth, and You have made me in Your image." 🐞

I am fearfully and wonderfully made… My frame was not hidden from You, when I was made in secret.
Psalm 139:14-15

There are times when you'll be in the middle of an impossible situation. It will seem as though trouble is coming at you from all sides. Look above. Speak to your own mind, heart, and soul the truth about your protector, Elohim. 🐞

I will say to the Lord, "My refuge and my fortress, my God [Elohim], in whom I trust!"
Psalm 91:2

There is so much that you try to take care of on your own. Do you realize you are not intended to carry your burden? Give it over to God, for you are in need of rest and help. Your reliance on God when you are weak or when you stumble reveals His very existence to the world. 🐞

The Everlasting God, the Lord, the Creator of the ends of the earth does not become weary or tired…He gives strength to the weary, and to him who lacks might He increases power.
Isaiah 40:28-29

Are you afraid because you've been let down by others and your heart is hardened or fragile? Does your need for help and strength cause you to feel alone in this world? You can turn to Elohim, who is always here for you. 🐞

Do not fear, for I am with you; do not anxiously look about you, for I am your God. I will strengthen you, surely I will help you, surely I will uphold you with My righteous right hand.
Isaiah 41:10

Delight in Elohim

Imagine God flinging the stars out in the universe and speaking planets into existence. Think about Him forming a human being from the dust of the earth and then breathing life into His creation. Contemplate His ability to breathe life into your impossible circumstance, whatever it may be. God, the uncreated, eternal, all-powerful, mighty, and majestic Creator, is greater than any obstacle you face today. You can rely on Him, the Designer of the universe and the human body, to weave a design into your life even when your circumstances may seem to be as formless and empty as the earth was prior to the completion of Elohim's work.

When you contemplate God, you step onto the ground of the incomprehensible and contemplate what you cannot wrap your mind around. Do not be afraid, dear friend. Venture onward into the vast, unfathomable land of God and look with awe and wonder. ❦

The LORD your God is the God of gods and the Lord of lords, the great, the mighty, and the awesome God.

Deuteronomy 10:17

Elohim, You are my foundation. In this life, the unknowns are so many and the certainties so few. But there is comfort and security each time I call out Your name, each time I seek strength, each time I hunger for Your presence. You lift me up. You hold me close. Your power transforms my weaknesses into possibilities. I give You praise today and tomorrow, for You are worthy, generous, and forever my Lord. Amen.

Draw Strength from El Elyon —He Is Your Sovereign

Blessed be Abram of God Most High, possessor of heaven and earth; and blessed be God Most High, who has delivered your enemies into your hand.

Genesis 14:19-20

Who is the one you can count on when everyone and everything seems to be working against you? Who is in charge of your life? His name is El Elyon. God revealed Himself as El Elyon to Abram following Abram's great victory over his enemies. From this deliverance, Abram knew El Elyon as his God, sovereign and supreme over every detail of his life, including his battles.

In your life, just like in Abram's, El Elyon reveals He is sovereign, He is in control, and He rules over all things. El Elyon has the power and might to change people, events, and circumstances right now and in the future. Whatever the scope of your troubles, you can take them to El Elyon and then watch, wait, and see what He will do in His perfect time. 🐦

His dominion is an eternal dominion;
his kingdom endures from generation to generation.

Daniel 4:34 NIV

Draw Near to El Elyon

Are you doubting the sovereignty and rule of God in your life? Do you keep a tight hold on your life rather than give it and your troubles to God? It's okay to release your grip. In fact, that is exactly what God is asking you to do. Take your worries, your need for control, and your struggles to the Lord and offer the prayer of David to your El Elyon. ❦

Yours, O Lord, is the greatness and the power and the glory and the victory and the majesty, indeed everything that is in the heavens and the earth; Yours is the dominion, O Lord, and You exalt Yourself as head over all. Both riches and honor come from You, and You rule over all, and in Your hand is power and might; and it lies in Your hand to make great and to strengthen everyone.
1 Chronicles 29:11-12

When you are discouraged about the lack of answers for your life, are you tempted to trust a sense of fate or luck? The offerings of the world are empty and misleading. If you worry about tomorrow or are even looking at today with the eyes of a skeptic, speak God's truths and stand in them. Remember who El Elyon is and rest in what He can do. ❦

I will cry to God Most High [El Elyon], to God who accomplishes all things for me.
Psalm 57:2

Have others done you harm? Have your own failures left a trail of pain? Take comfort in this: God is greater than those who intend evil, and He is certainly greater than our failing hearts. Be ready for the greatness of El Elyon's purpose for your life. ❦

God causes all things to work together for good to those who love God, to those who are called according to His purpose.
Romans 8:28

Do you have an overwhelming burden that consumes your life? Is your financial situation a mess? Do you have difficulties in your relationships? Many people spend days, months, and even years complaining about their plight. There is no need to carry your troubles—or spread them around—for so long. Wait no longer to take your problems to El Elyon. ❧

He who dwells in the shelter of the Most High will rest in the shadow of the Almighty. I will say of the Lord, "He is my refuge and my fortress, my God, in whom I trust."

Psalm 91:1-2 NIV

Delight in El Elyon

When I realized I had agonized about two difficult situations for more than three years, I took these all-consuming problems to El Elyon and prayed some very specific requests. Within a week, dramatic events occurred, changing both those prolonged difficulties for the better. I learned a powerful lesson about trusting El Elyon.

Let them know that you, whose name is the Lord—that you alone are the Most High over all the earth.

Psalm 83:18 NIV

If you have a problem with the way things are going in your life, take it up with the Lord. Remember, He can change hearts. He can find new jobs. He can mend brokenness. He can remove obstacles. Resolve to live your life in the light of El Elyon, your sovereign God. And don't be surprised if the greatest change takes place right inside of you—how you think and how you walk with God. Sometimes He will deliver you. Sometimes He will use you in a surprisingly powerful way in your present circumstances, giving you strength and wisdom. And sometimes He will dramatically change the course of your life. ❧

El Elyon, You are the one true God, the sovereign ruler of the heavens and the earth. I give to You all of me and my life. I seek Your deliverance from my troubles, my failings, and my desire for control. You have the power to change circumstances, hearts, minds, and lives. I am excited to see my life transformed by Your hands and Your will. As You shape my days, I will praise You, El Elyon. Amen.

Draw Strength from Adonai
—He Is Your Lord

I heard the voice of the Lord saying, "Whom shall I send? And who will go for us?" And I said, "Here am I. Send me!"

Isaiah 6:8 NIV

The world presents many masters we can be tempted to follow. They can capture our attention and our hearts. We can choose which ambition to pursue, which master to serve, and which agenda to respond to. To serve the living God, we must say yes to His lordship in our lives. We must say yes to Adonai. When Adonai is the one we follow, He is our motivation, our master, our owner, and our mentor.

Many years ago I pledged, "Lord, my name is Catherine. Here I am. Send me." That declaration signified a commitment from me to say, "Adonai, You are my Lord and Master." To this day, I know whose I am—His, forever. If our desire is to belong to God and to be faithful, we discover that for our lives to be saved and transformed, we are called to give our lives completely to Adonai. Spend time with your Lord and discover the plans He has for you. ❦

If anyone wishes to come after Me, he must deny himself, and take up his cross and follow Me. For whoever wishes to save his life will lose it; but whoever loses his life for My sake will find it.

Matthew 16:24-25

Draw Near to Adonai

Has someone who was in authority in your life ever led without compassion? When you question the idea of submitting to anyone or anything, even the Master, consider that a good master will protect, help, teach, and direct his servant. Adonai is master and owner of those who love their master so much so that they are servants for life. Walk toward Him and toward submission. Trust in Adonai.

You call Me Teacher and Lord; and you are right, for so I am.

John 13:13

When you are at a crossroads and want to know which way to go, call on Adonai. Do you feel the tug of the world more than the tug of God's leading? Do not settle for the riches of man and remain poor in spirit. Choose Adonai as your one master and you will experience the direction and freedom you desire.

No one can serve two masters; for either he will hate the one and love the other, or he will be devoted to one and despise the other. You cannot serve God and wealth.

Matthew 6:24

The world shows us many images of what it looks like to serve ourselves. But if you want to understand what being a servant of God looks like, if you want to understand what it means to serve Adonai, look at the example of Jesus and how He lived His life on earth.

[Jesus] made himself nothing, taking the very nature of a servant, being made in human likeness. And being found in appearance as a man, he humbled himself and became obedient to death—even death on a cross!

Philippians 2:7-8 NIV

When you hunger for purpose and meaning, you need sustenance that feeds the soul. When Adonai fills you, you are filled forever. Good works and truths will flow out of this plenty. Follow the way of Jesus and serve Adonai with that hunger in your heart. Let Him fill you and guide you so that the work of your hands, mind, and soul is pleasing, honorable, and of service to your Lord.

My food is to do the will of Him who sent Me and to accomplish His work.

John 4:34

Delight in Adonai

The greatest blessing of all is to serve God. Adonai has given you time, talents, and treasure. Your trust and reliance on God means you will submit to Him, serve Him, and act as a good steward of all He entrusts to you. In fact, if you have said yes to Adonai, your whole life is dedicated to serving your Lord.

Don't hold back. Run to Him and cry out, "Adonai, here I am. I delight to do Your will. Send me where You will. Use me how You will. Mold me as You will." He is looking for those servants who will say, "Here I am." Take delight in serving Adonai, and the course of your life and the state of your heart will be transformed forever. 🍂

His master said to him, "Well done, good and faithful slave. You were faithful with a few things, I will put you in charge of many things; enter into the joy of your master."

Matthew 25:21

Adonai, I no longer belong to myself. I belong to You alone. I have been bought with a price—the life of Jesus. I give to You, Adonai, the rights to my possessions, to my job, my relationships, my past, and my future. I am Your servant. May all that I say and do serve the purpose You have for me. I love You and will walk humbly with You forever. Amen.

Draw Strength from El Shaddai
—He Is Enough for You

When Abram was ninety-nine years old, the Lord appeared to him and said, "I am God Almighty; walk before me and be blameless." Genesis 17:1 NIV

God is not distant. He interacts with us. He initiates a personal, intimate, vibrant relationship. Genesis 17:1 says the Lord appeared to Abram and spoke to him. God makes His presence known and also speaks—two vital actions for any relationship. When Abram met El Shaddai, he became a friend of God.

God is so much more than you know. By turning to and leaning on El Shaddai, you discover that He has the power to fulfill His promises. By giving your needs to El Shaddai, you will experience His power—the power of an almighty God who has a never-ending bounty for His people. El Shaddai brings you to the place of abundance where you experience a renewal of relationship with your Creator. Call on your friend El Shaddai. ❦

Call to me and I will answer you and tell you great and unsearchable things you do not know.

Jeremiah 33:3 NIV

Draw Near to El Shaddai

When you are weary from trying to do everything in your own power, consider what knowing El Shaddai tells you about yourself. You need Him. God abundantly supplies grace, goodness, mercy, kindness, strength, and comfort— whatever your need may be. Face your obstacles with this truth: The power of El Shaddai is in your life because Jesus now lives in you. He is enough. ❦

I have been crucified with Christ and I no longer live, but Christ lives in me. The life I live in the body, I live by faith in the Son of God, who loved me and gave himself for me.
Galatians 2:20-21 NIV

When you feel overwhelmed by a roadblock of obstacles up ahead, don't follow the instinct to run in the other direction. Take a step toward the problem. The greater the obstacle, the more you will experience Christ. Enter the valley or start your climb. Strength will come as you move forward with the power of El Shaddai. ❦

He has said to me, "My grace is sufficient for you, for power is perfected in weakness."
2 Corinthians 12:9

When you doubt whether you have enough of what it takes to persevere in daily tasks, El Shaddai will inspire you to be a person of great endurance. When you trust in El Shaddai, you will learn to never give up as you watch God match your need with His suffciency, regardless of the depth of the challenge. ❦

Ah Lord God! Behold, You have made the heavens and the earth by Your great power and by Your outstretched arm! Nothing is too difficult for You.
Jeremiah 32:17

Do you have a sense of purpose, but wonder if you have what it takes to fulfill it? Whether your calling is a great ministry, a great responsibility, or a great suffering, the good work God has started in you will be completed in the power of El Shaddai. ❦

God is able to make all grace abound to you, so that in all things at all times, having all that you need, you will abound in every good work.
2 Corinthians 9:8 NIV

Delight in El Shaddai

Meeting El Shaddai will light the fire of devotion in your heart. Drawing near to El Shaddai will make you a radical disciple in your generation. Loving El Shaddai will set you apart from many in your culture as you dare to do mighty things in His power. When El Shaddai calls you to Himself, He will inspire you to great tasks…and sometimes even great sorrows.

To him who is able to do immeasurably more than all we ask or imagine, according to his power that is at work within us, to him be glory in the church and in Christ Jesus throughout all generations, for ever and ever! Amen.

Ephesians 3:20-21 NIV

When El Shaddai makes His presence known and speaks to you, He inspires you to amazing prayer because God expects us to ask Him for remarkable things. When you realize that nothing is too difficult for God, you will trust Him for even seemingly impossible things. You will walk by faith with your eyes fixed on El Shaddai and not on the obstacles in your life.

Delighting in El Shaddai today means worshipping with your entire life, bowing your heart in sheer reverence to almighty God, the powerful One, who has unlimited supply and is able to do beyond all we ask. How will El Shaddai change your life? 🌿

El Shaddai, in my times of sorrow, joy, hardship, and doubt, You make Your presence known. You speak promises into my life, and You fulfill every one. I used to be timid about coming to You with my needs and dreams, but now I have a courageous faith. I am so grateful I am able to witness the mighty things You do and the mighty God You are. Amen.

Draw Strength from Yahweh Jireh —He Is Your Provider

My God will supply all your needs according to His riches in glory in Christ Jesus.

Philippians 4:19

Abraham faced his greatest trial when he was asked to sacrifice his son Isaac. But on that day and in that place, Abraham met Yahweh Jireh, who provided a sacrifice and spared the boy. All of us have Isaacs that must be placed on the altar—a dream, a loved one, our health, a job, or financial security. These surrenders often test our faith. In a test, what you know to be true in the Bible is challenged by how you feel, what you think, or what you see happening in your life circumstances.

Trusting in Yahweh Jireh carries you to the other side of tests of faith. Yahweh Jireh gives you hope blended with faith, and the result is TRUST: Total Reliance Under Stress and Trial. Where do you turn when your faith is tested to the brink of failure, to the point of doubting what God has promised? Discover that what He has said He will do—the Lord will provide. 🦋

Abraham called the name of that place The Lord Will Provide.

Genesis 22:14

Draw Near to Yahweh Jireh

When it is difficult to rest in your trial because you feel too scattered, too anxious, or too fearful, turn your attention to the blessings that come with tests of faith. Are you more dependent on God? Are you actively seeking His provision? Consider this difficult time to be your invitation to know Yahweh Jireh personally. ❧

In this you greatly rejoice, though now for a little while you may have had to suffer grief in all kinds of trials. These have come so that your faith—of greater worth than gold, which perishes even though refined by fire—may be proved genuine and may result in praise, glory and honor when Jesus Christ is revealed.

1 Peter 1:6-7 NIV

When you are in the middle of a life storm and you cannot make sense of it, Yahweh Jireh sees you and provides for your needs. There will be times when you cannot understand the *why* behind a circumstance, but you can come to understand *who* will provide the strength for and the way through that circumstance—Yahweh Jireh. ❧

As the heavens are higher than the earth, so are My ways higher than your ways and My thoughts than your thoughts.

Isaiah 55:9

Do you feel alone in your hardship and your pain? Do you wonder who can understand the ache that is in your heart or the loss you have experienced? Look to Yahweh Jireh's heart. He cares about your struggle and provides hope, comfort, and encouragement when you are feeling pain. Look to Yahweh Jireh and see His compassion for you. It flows deeply. It flows for you. ❧

This I call to mind and therefore I have hope: Because of the LORD's great love we are not consumed, for his compassions never fail. They are new every morning; great is your faithfulness.

Lamentations 3:21-23 NIV

When you question how you are going to make it, when you doubt the truth of God's Word, or when you wonder how God can help you in your crisis, you must run to Yahweh Jireh, asking Him for direction and faith. He will give you eyes to see the gifts that fill the void a sacrifice leaves in your life—perseverance, character, and hope.

Since we have been justified through faith, we have peace with God through our Lord Jesus Christ, through whom we have gained access by faith into this grace in which we now stand. And we rejoice in the hope of the glory of God. Not only so, but we also rejoice in our sufferings, because we know that suffering produces perseverance; perseverance, character; and character, hope. And hope does not disappoint us, because God has poured out his love into our hearts by the Holy Spirit, whom he has given us.

Romans 5:1-5 NIV

Delight in Yahweh Jireh

How do you respond when God asks the seemingly impossible of you? The impossible becomes possible when you know and trust in Yahweh Jireh. Our greatest tests of faith rapidly exhaust every possible resource, forcing us to look upon God's provision as our only hope. You can spend many fruitless years looking elsewhere for security and answers, but a trial connects you quickly to God's promises if you'll let it. Is there hope in your time of loss or difficulty, whatever it may be? Yes, because the Lord promises He will provide for you.

Trusting in God's promises when you cannot imagine how He will carry out His plan demonstrates to Him your great faith. When God sees this great faith, He provides in the most amazing and miraculous ways.

The God of all grace, who called you to his eternal glory in Christ, after you have suffered a little while, will himself restore you and make you strong, firm and steadfast. To him be the power for ever and ever. Amen.

1 Peter 5:10-11 NIV

Yahweh Jireh, You know my fears, doubts, and questions. I am coming to You, the One who has provided for Your children throughout the ages. I ask You to provide all I need in this testing of my faith. Life is so confusing that I don't even know how to identify what my needs are. I entrust these uncertainties and my future to Your hands. Amen.

Draw Strength from El Ro'i
—He Sees You

"You are the God who sees me. . . I have now seen the One who sees me." That is why the well was called Beer Lahai Roi.

Genesis 16:13-14 NIV

To be seen and known is a simple but incredibly powerful need that exists in all of God's children. Hagar, an Egyptian maidservant, was harshly treated and fled to the desert twice, fearing for her life. She was scared and alone. Both times the angel of the Lord saw Hagar's distress and comforted her. Who is this God who would meet an outcast servant in the desert? He is the same God who will meet you in your wilderness experience—El Ro'i.

Regardless of how desperate, abandoned, or distant you feel, God will find you and He will comfort you. El Ro'i witnesses all that you do and understands all that you are. Your human desire to be known is met by the One who sees you. ❧

The eye of the Lord is on those who fear Him, on those who hope for His lovingkindness, to deliver their soul from death and to keep them alive in famine.

Psalm 33:18-19

Draw Near to El Ro'i

Are there times when you think nobody notices the real you or the efforts you make to reach out? El Ro'i notices everything about you. When you call out to El Ro'i, it is not to get His attention, for His eyes are already upon you. It is to connect with the God who is waiting there for you. 🐞

The LORD your God is the one who goes with you. He will not fail you or forsake you.

Deuteronomy 31:6

Is life one big mystery? Have you been thrown by complicated circumstances or deceptions of the world? When we meditate on El Ro'i, we are venturing into the incomprehensible mystery of God's omniscience, His infinite knowledge and wisdom. Nothing is a mystery to God. Nothing is a problem to God. No puzzles can cloud God's mind. Rest in the all-knowing El Ro'i. 🐞

Oh, the depth of the riches of the wisdom and knowledge of God! How unsearchable his judgments, and his paths beyond tracing out! Who has known the mind of the Lord? Or who has been his counselor? Who has ever given to God, that God should repay him? For from him and through him and to him are all things. To him be the glory forever!

Romans 11:33-36 NIV

Do people tend to see only what you can do for them rather than your needs and hurts? God does not see as man sees—superficially, incompletely, and impassively. When you feel invisible and insignificant in your quest for direction or justice or wholeness, El Ro'i sees your plight and will act on your behalf; He will not abandon you. 🐞

God sees not as man sees, for man looks at the outward appearance, but the LORD looks at the heart.

1 Samuel 16:7

In your past, you've undoubtedly been hurt. Do you long to know that God saw those people who did the hurting, the betraying? Let go of your past pains to His care and at the same time, release those who tried to break you. God's vision is vast, limitless, and constant. He did not miss that moment or those times of heartache. He saw the loss, and now El Ro'i is here to see your healing. 🐞

The LORD said, "I have surely seen the affliction of My people. . .I am aware of their sufferings."

Exodus 3:7

Delight in El Ro'i

Civilla Martin and her husband were sojourning in Elmira, New York, in the spring of 1905. They became friends with a Mr. and Mrs. Doolittle, a joyful couple even though Mrs. Doolittle had been bedridden for 20 years, and her husband was restricted to a wheelchair. One day Civilla asked Mrs. Doolittle the secret of her hopefulness. The woman's reply was simply, "His eye is on the sparrow, and I know He watches me." Civilla Martin penned a poem and mailed it to Charles Gabriel, who supplied the music to what became a beloved song.

Are not two sparrows sold for a penny? Yet not one of them will fall to the ground apart from the will of your Father. And even the very hairs of your head are all numbered. So don't be afraid; you are worth more than many sparrows.

Matthew 10:29-31 NIV

Delighting in El Ro'i means you praise Him for His presence, His person, His protection, and His perception. Always remember that as His eye is on the sparrow, so His eye is on you.

The human experience will lead you through lonely deserts and the wilderness of uncertainty. When you think about Ro'i, think about the very presence of God. You are not alone. And God never meant for you to be alone—He is your great Companion in life. 🐦

El Ro'i, You are the One who sees me. Such peace comes over me when I realize that You will not forget me. You have engraved me on the palms of Your hands. I am continually before You. My needs and my praises are always in Your ear. And my desire to be seen and known is quenched in my relationship with You, El Ro'i. Amen.

Draw Strength from Yahweh
—He Is Everything You Need

Jesus said to them, "Truly, truly, I say to you, before Abraham was born, I am."

John 8:58

Jesus declared for all to hear, "I am." He proclaimed to those standing before Him that He existed before Abraham and was greater than Abraham. He was telling them that they were His and He was their God. He was all they needed. They were in the presence of Yahweh.

Trust Yahweh as He leads you to the most sacred, holy place in your relationship with Him. However personal and intimate God is with us, His very being and presence command sheer reverence, utter respect, and absolute worship. He is God and Creator. And yet He speaks. He invites. He touches. He enters our lives. He initiates. He is insistent and persistent. He is personal.

Whatever your circumstance, however much you have cried out to God, and wherever your suffering occurs, He sees, He hears, and He knows. And when Yahweh acts, He delivers a definitive response. Discover the faithfulness and provision of Yahweh. 🍇

"Shout and be glad, O Daughter of Zion. For I am coming, and I will live among you," declares the LORD. "Many nations will be joined with the LORD in that day and will become my people. I will live among you and you will know that the Lord Almighty has sent me to you."

Zechariah 2:10-11 NIV

Draw Near to Yahweh

When your personal connection with God falters, when you look about and do not feel the presence of God, look to Yahweh. He lives with you. He reaches out to you. He shows you your heavenly Father. Come to know Yahweh, and you will know the heart of God for you. ❦

Have you entrusted your deepest needs to God? Do you hold back and then wonder why you don't experience a life transformed? Remain in Yahweh and your life will bear His righteous fruit. ❦

Does your patience run thin? Are you spending your days looking for evidence of God's favor rather than spending your days in relationship with Yahweh? God always works according to His own plan and time frame. With perfect timing, He breaks into history and works in powerful ways in the lives of His people. Wait in and with Yahweh to discover His ways. ❦

Has fear been instilled in your heart by people who are quick to anger, eager to blame? If your relationships have lacked love, patience, kindness, forgiveness, and honesty, you have not yet witnessed the personal relationship offered to you by Yahweh. Let go of the model you have experienced and embrace the intimate communion that awaits in the arms of Yahweh. ❦

Philip said, "Lord, show us the Father and that will be enough for us." Jesus answered: "Don't you know me, Philip, even after I have been among you such a long time? Anyone who has seen me has seen the Father. How can you say, 'Show us the Father'?"

John 14:8-9 NIV

I am the vine; you are the branches. If a man remains in me and I in him, he will bear much fruit; apart from me you can do nothing.

John 15:5-6 NIV

If I have found favor in Your sight, let me know Your ways that I may know You, so that I may find favor in your sight.

Exodus 33:13

The Lord, the Lord God, compassionate and gracious, slow to anger, and abounding in lovingkindness and truth; who keeps lovingkindness for thousands, who forgives iniquity, transgression, and sin.

Exodus 34:6-7

Delight in Yahweh

I stood in the Sistine Chapel in the Vatican, lifting my gaze for a view of Michelangelo's magnificent rendering of God and Adam. God reaches out His finger with the spark of life toward the outstretched hand of Adam! My first thought was, *Amazing—a personal God who reaches out to me and desires a relationship with me.*

God said to Moses, "I AM who I AM. This is what you are to say to the Israelites: I AM has sent me to you."

Exodus 3:14 NIV

Yahweh reaches out to you. Spend private, personal, intimate quiet time alone with Him and discover His love for you. Listen to what He says to you in His Word, and talk with Him about everything on your heart. Yahweh has all the answers and holds the keys to everything you face. He is not worried. He is not wondering what He is going to do. He is delighted when you confidently seek Him.

Rejoice in the gift of touch and connection with your Savior. He loves you. Nothing can separate you from His love. He is always with you, and He will never leave you or forsake you.

Yahweh, I praise You and my heart rejoices with the desire to worship You. Only You have filled me with a truth about love and compassion. When I met You, I did not have confidence or direction. But You said You would be my God, Yahweh, and You have replaced my needs with promises. You have shown me the truth and beauty of personal, eternal love. Amen.

Draw Strength from Yahweh Rophe —He Is Your Healer

I, the LORD, am your healer.

Exodus 15:26

When the people of Israel had traveled for days without water and then came upon a source that provided bitter water, they grumbled. But Moses prayed. And the Lord revealed Himself to Moses as Yahweh Rophe, the God who heals. He made the bitter waters sweet so the people could quench their thirst.

Are you in need of healing today? Do you have a broken heart, a wounded soul, or a physical illness or disability? Declare the name of Yahweh Rophe and take your needs to Him. He is your comfort in such desperate times. Yahweh Rophe changed the waters from bitter to sweet for the people of Israel; He can change your pain and disappointment, giving you a new view of God Himself so that you may trust Him more.

Go to Yahweh Rophe. Cry out to Him and taste the sweetness of healing. ❧

Heal me, O LORD, and I will be healed; save me and I will be saved.

Jeremiah 17:14

Draw Near to Yahweh Rophe

Are you going through difficulties you have never faced before? Don't sink into the pain. Seek God's Word and His deliverance. Call out to Yahweh Rophe. Give Him your pain and your praise. ❧

When you need spiritual, physical, and emotional healing, do you feel as though you've failed? During those nights when you cry out for God's help, do you do it with reluctance or shame or guilt? Allow yourself to fully, truly rest in the compassion of the Great Physician. Yahweh Rophe is here for you. ❧

Discouragement and depression can weigh down your heart and soul. Are you ready to be released from that burden? Turn to Yahweh Rophe during your time of longing. Ask to be filled with His hope. Ask to be saved by His love. ❧

Then they cried to the Lord in their trouble, and he saved them from their distress. He sent forth his word and healed them; he rescued them from the grave. Let them give thanks to the Lord for his unfailing love and his wonderful deeds for men.

Psalm 107:19-20 NIV

Jesus said to them, "It is not those who are healthy who need a physician, but those who are sick; I did not come to call the righteous, but sinners."

Mark 2:17

Be gracious to me, O Lord, for I am pining away; heal me, O Lord, for my bones are dismayed. And my soul is greatly dismayed; but You, O Lord—how long? Return, O Lord, rescue my soul; save me because of Your lovingkindness.

Psalm 6:2-4

Has your suffering lasted a long time? Is it hard to see past the pain of today to a brighter tomorrow? When you place your suffering in the merciful hands of Yahweh Rophe, you will taste His peace in the midst of your struggle. Hold onto the hope

that beyond the mountains of obstacles you endure in this life is a beautiful land, your eternal home with God. 🌿

I heard a loud voice from the throne saying, "Now the dwelling of God is with men, and he will live with them. They will be his people, and God himself will be with them and be their God. He will wipe every tear from their eyes. There will be no more death or mourning or crying or pain, for the old order of things has passed away."

Revelation 21:3-4 NIV

Delight in Yahweh Rophe

We experience healing every day of our lives, and most of the time, our healing goes unnoticed and unrecognized. God Himself created the amazing design of the human body and its ability to fight diseases and infections. This is the power of Yahweh Rophe, the Lord your healer.

He counts the number of the stars; He gives names to all of them. Great is our Lord and abundant in strength; His understanding is infinite. The LORD supports the afflicted.

Psalm 147:3-6

We face many trials and afflictions—physical, emotional, and spiritual infirmities, but you can place your trust in Yahweh Rophe. Just as our brokenness and frailty take many forms, so can our healing. Sometimes Yahweh Rophe's healing is within your heart, strengthening you to face your difficulty with a new endurance. You can learn to trust as you rely on God's names and then wait patiently to see what He will accomplish. Can God heal? Yes. Will He heal? Yes, He is Yahweh Rophe. The Lord is the Great Physician. But how and when will He heal? We cannot presume to know. Watch and wait to see how He heals. And trust Yahweh Rophe. 🌿

Yahweh Rophe, I am so thankful that I have You as my refuge. When my needs are great, I know that Your ability to heal is greater. Help me to recognize the healing that You are doing in my life. Your mercy covers me. Your comfort spares me from the pain of loneliness and isolation. May the world see that where I am lacking, hurting, or failing...Your strength is abundant. Amen.

Draw Strength from Yahweh Shalom
—He Is Your Peace

The Lord said to him, "Peace! Do not be afraid. You are not going to die." So Gideon built an altar to the Lord there and called it "The Lord is Peace."

Judges 6:23-24 NIV

Gideon and his people, the Israelites, were hiding in the mountains from their enemies. Gideon felt abandoned and defeated. So when he first heard from God, his doubt was strong. But he encountered God as Yahweh Shalom, the Lord of Peace, and doubt gave way to belief. He was given a deep, abiding peace and became a mighty warrior. He tore down idols, worshipped God, and accomplished great things.

Trusting Yahweh Shalom gives you a new view of adversity. God has not abandoned you in your trouble. Rather, He may be leading you into a new place of influence and fulfillment. Gideon learned that peace was more than a feeling or a state of being, but was and is the Lord Himself. Turn to Yahweh Shalom. Experience the peace of God that is like a mighty river flowing deep in your heart, changing you, guiding you, and leading you to do great things in the name of God. ❧

The LORD gives strength to his people; the LORD blesses his people with peace.

Psalm 29:11 NIV

Draw Near to Yahweh Shalom

When you wander through your days with a restless heart, you will be tempted to follow worldly tangents and temporary pleasures rather than God's truth. But when you focus on Yahweh Shalom, His peace will direct your steps. Entertain the perspective that God is calling you to a higher standard and a greater purpose. Let fear and trouble fall away as you carry the peace of Yahweh Shalom confidently toward that purpose. 🐞

Do you encounter conflict at home or the workplace? Can you sense the air of rebellion in your own family? It's time to walk in the peace of Yahweh Shalom. Share this peace with those in your life through your actions, words, and priorities. Call out to Yahweh Shalom each day. Seek the covering of His peace in every situation. 🐞

If you turn from God during a hardship, your journey will become lonely and filled with silence. Gideon was in that silence until he met Yahweh Shalom. Then he became a man of prayer, talking constantly with God, and God spoke constantly with him. Break your silence. You will discover that you are not alone but are being drawn nearer to God's heart during your difficulty. 🐞

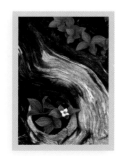

Though the storm of anxiety rages about you, His peace keeps you secure and calm in Him. Trust in His power and strength to pull you through the tempest. Give your praise and troubles to Yahweh Shalom. 🐞

Peace I leave with you; My peace I give to you; not as the world gives do I give to you. Do not let your heart be troubled, nor let it be fearful.
John 14:27

May the Lord of peace Himself continually grant you peace in every circumstance. The Lord be with you all!
2 Thessalonians 3:16

He came and preached peace to you who were far away and peace to those who were near. For through him we both have access to the Father by one Spirit.
Ephesians 2:17-18 NIV

Be anxious for nothing, but in everything by prayer and supplication with thanksgiving let your requests be made known to God. And the peace of God, which surpasses all comprehension, will guard your hearts and your minds in Christ Jesus.
Philippians 4:6-7

Delight in Yahweh Shalom

Perhaps you have heard the story of the artist who was commissioned by a wealthy man to paint a depiction of peace. He first painted a peaceful country scene and then the serenity of a sleeping baby, but both submissions were rejected by his benefactor. Finally, after much thought, he prayed for inspiration from God. Suddenly, an idea came to him; he painted with unrestrained purpose and zeal. When his employer studied the

finished painting, he looked at the artist and said, "Now this is a picture of true peace." And what was the painting? The fury of a stormy sea striking a rugged cliff. But under the cliff, snuggled safely in its nest, was a small bird, at peace though the stormed raged.

We can delight in the security of Yahweh Shalom even amid life's storms. Whatever your trouble, learn to take it to the Lord in prayer. What strength you will have as peace keeps watch over your heart, maintaining your faith, courage, and boldness as you face the storm before you. ❦

He arose and rebuked the wind, and said to the sea, "Peace, be still!" And the wind ceased and there was a great calm.

Mark 4:39 NKJV

Yahweh Shalom, thank You for being my peace. You have a plan and will accomplish what needs to take place in my circumstances. When I have shalom in my life, my direction and calling become clear. I want to see the mighty purpose You have for me. No longer will I pull back from talking with You, but I will seek Your face and celebrate my relationship with the Lord who is peace. Amen.

Draw Strength from Yahweh Ro'i
—He Is Your Shepherd

The Lord is my shepherd, I shall not want.

Psalm 23:1

Do you sometimes become overwhelmed by your needs and responsibilities? Whether you are caring for your family, leading a ministry or business, or handling a difficult trial, there is One greater than you ready to guide you. In the book of Psalms, David introduces us to *the* Shepherd, Yahweh Ro'i. How fitting that David, a man after God's own heart, would be given the privilege to present the Lord as our Shepherd. For who could define the tenderness of the Shepherd better than David, a man who knew the relationship of a shepherd to his sheep, having watched over his own flocks, both in the fields and as king of the people of Israel.

When you encounter and come to know Yahweh Ro'i, you will want for nothing. The Lord is *your* Shepherd. He meets all of your needs, gives you rest, leads you, restores you, makes you righteous, comforts you, keeps you from fear, protects you from your enemies, gives you overflowing and abundant life, and leads you to the springs of eternal life. 🐑

The Lamb at the center of the throne will be their shepherd; he will lead them to springs of living water.

Revelation 7:17 NIV

Draw Near to Yahweh Ro'i

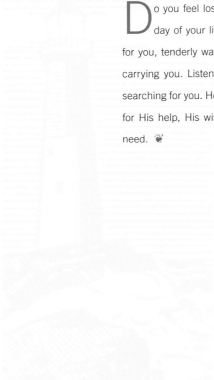

Do you feel lost? Draw near to Yahweh Ro'i every day of your life, for He is your Shepherd, caring for you, tenderly watching over you, and at times even carrying you. Listen closely. When you are lost, He is searching for you. He is calling out to you. Respond. Ask for His help, His wisdom, and His care for your every need. ❧

Have you been juggling multiple priorities for so long that you don't know which way to turn? Are there demands of the world clamoring for your constant attention? Focus on the voice of your Shepherd. Stay close to Him and don't let anything or anyone pull you away from following Him. ❧

What concerns hold you back from trusting God? The Shepherd loves His sheep so much that He will lay down His own life to save them. Trust Yahweh Ro'i. He has come so that you might follow Him completely and faithfully. ❧

I myself will search for my sheep and look after them. As a shepherd looks after his scattered flock when he is with them, so will I look after my sheep. I will rescue them from all the places where they were scattered on a day of clouds and darkness.

Ezekiel 34:11-12 NIV

The watchman opens the gate for him, and the sheep listen to his voice. He calls his own sheep by name and leads them out. When he has brought out all his own, he goes on ahead of them, and his sheep follow him because they know his voice. But they will never follow a stranger; in fact, they will run away from him because they do not recognize a stranger's voice.

John 10:3-5 NIV

I am the good shepherd; I know my sheep and my sheep know me—just as the Father knows me and I know the Father—and I lay down my life for the sheep.

John 10:14-15 NIV

Fear can hold us back from following the way of the Shepherd when we face uncertainties. What fears keep you awake

at night? When you have a need, run to your Shepherd. If you are in trouble, call out to your Shepherd. There is nothing He cannot handle. 🐑

God has said, "Never will I leave you; never will I forsake you." So we say with confidence, "The Lord is my helper; I will not be afraid. What can man do to me?"

Hebrews 13:5-6 NIV

Delight in Yahweh Ro'i

My friend Shirley tells the story of her Aunt Sally who cared for four little lambs. She nurtured them and called them throughout the day by their names: Buckaroo, Lefty, Fluffy, and Stumpy. When summer came, she reluctantly let them join the flock to go with the ranch hands to the pasture.

At the end of summer, Sally heard the sheep coming home. She rushed to the fence and began calling her own by name. One by one, three sheep came to her. She called the fourth again, but Lefty's ears had grown deaf to the voice of his shepherdess. You will be blessed when you are like the three sheep—able to discern the voice of Yahweh Ro'i.

When Jesus speaks of His relationship with His sheep, He points to the intimacy He has with those who belong to Him. Delight in the Shepherd's presence and His promises. You will find comfort in His arms. You will find purpose and love in His instruction. And you will discover the great gift of belonging to Yahweh Ro'i. 🐑

I am the good shepherd, and I know My own and My own know Me.

John 10:14

Yahweh Ro'i, thank You for being my Shepherd. Thank You for promising to search for me, seek me out, care for me, feed me, and deliver me. I know You will carry me when I cannot walk and lead me when I am unsure of my way. I trust You with my very life. Amen.

Draw Strength from Abba, Father
—He Is Your Father

"Abba, Father," he said, "everything is possible for you. Take this cup from me. Yet not what I will, but what you will."

Mark 14:36 NIV

Do you ever doubt your future, your value, or question your significance? Rest in this wonderful truth: You have great significance because you are a child of God. In His time of need in the garden of Gethsemane, Jesus cries out to Abba, Father. This name for God is used in the spirit of a tender, affectionate child. It is calling out "Daddy." Abba reveals the most intimate of all father–child relationships. And you are given that same tender, personal, and blessed relationship with God. Isn't that amazing?

Because He is your Abba, Father, you may call to Him with such an expression of affection, and you may be assured of what this name of God says about you— you are His child. You are part of the family of God. Don't ever forget who you are and *whose* you are. ❦

O righteous Father, although the world has not known You, yet I have known You.

John 17:25

Draw Near to Abba, Father

Is it hard to imagine what a close relationship with your heavenly Father looks like? Maybe you don't have an earthly example of such love? When Jesus repeatedly called God "My Father," it reflected a unique, intimate relationship with Him as His Son. It was radical for that time. The idea of such intimacy with God is just as radical and true today. Fall into His everlasting arms whispering *Papa, Daddy*. He longs for this relationship with you. He loves having you with Him. He wants to hear everything you say. Experience the privilege of calling out to Abba, Father. ❧

Have earthly relationships left you stranded? Does your heart thirst for acceptance and yet you struggle to express or accept love? Don't lose hope. Rejoice in your heritage as a child of God. Because of the compassion and grace of your Abba, Father, you have the privilege of swimming in the ocean of your Father's love. Dive in. ❧

When the world is overwhelming, draw near to your Father. Some of us bear tremendous burdens of responsibility or heavy loads of suffering. You may run into the throne room of God as children would run to their fathers or mothers. Lay every one of your needs, desires, difficulties—indeed, every request in His able hands. You have the privilege of prayer. Share your burdens with Abba, Father. ❧

Eternal life is all wrapped up in Jesus. His sacrifice leads to your inheritance. Such great love we have been offered through grace. The inheritance that is far beyond any earthly one is that of living in God's presence always. You are on a journey to discover God's character, His heart, and His love. What a gift that this journey continues as you live as a child of God. Celebrate the privilege of lasting life, lasting love, and a lasting relationship with Abba, Father. ❧

Because you are sons, God sent the Spirit of his Son into our hearts, the Spirit who calls out, "Abba, Father." So you are no longer a slave, but a son; and since you are a son, God has made you also an heir.
Galatians 4:6-7 NIV

See how great a love the Father has bestowed on us, that we would be called children of God; and such we are.
1 John 3:1

Let us draw near with confidence to the throne of grace, so that we may receive mercy and find grace to help in time of need.
Hebrews 4:16

God has given us eternal life, and this life is in His Son.
1 John 5:11

Delight in Abba, Father

When I think of delighting in Abba, Father, I think of an early morning ritual at my brother's house. My little niece, Kayla, runs into the room and crawls onto her daddy's lap, with her daddy's arms quickly pulling her close to his heart. Her daddy says, "Kayla, have I told you yet?"

Kayla says, "I know, Daddy."

"What do you know?"

"You love me."

Then her daddy says, "Kayla, your daddy loves you more than anything. I love you today, tomorrow, and always."

Dear friend, embrace your inheritance as a child of the One who is your Creator, your Sovereign, your Lord, Enough for you, your Provider, the One who sees you, Everything you need, your Healer, your Peace, your Shepherd, and *your* Father.

We have a future and hope because God is our Father and we are His children. One day we will stand face-to-face with Him and experience the reality of our relationship with God in a completely new way. Delight in being His child. ❧

> I will be their God and they will be my children.
>
> Revelation 21:7 TNIV

Abba, Father, thank You for calling me Your child. Such love is almost more than I can fathom, and yet I believe that You keep Your promises. When I call out to You and speak Your names, I am drawn closer to Your heart and Your love. I am Yours. Amen.

The LORD will give strength to His people;

The LORD will bless His people with peace.

Psalm 29:11